Sheep was the first to be seeker.

"I'm not looking," she said, as she started to count down from ten. "You all need to go and hide!"

Everyone quickly raced off to hide.

Duck hid in the duck pond. Chicken hid under a huge flower pot. Owl sat very still in his tree, hidden by the thick branches.

"3 - 2 - 1. Coming!" bleated Sheep. Then she trotted around the farm, looking for the hidden animals.

She spied Duck first.
"I can see you, Duck," she shrieked.

Duck flapped her wings and came out of hiding.

"Now you have to help me find the rest of the animals," Sheep told Duck.

Duck was not very good at finding.
"My birthday should be fun," she moaned.
"But this isn't fun!"

The next time they played, it was Duck's turn to be seeker.

Duck started to count down from ten. "You'd better all go and hide!" she yelled. "I'm not looking!"

But Duck was a cheat! She wasn't playing hide and seek. She was playing hide and **peek**!

As the animals raced off to hide, Duck peeked. She could see where all the animals were hiding.

"3 - 2 - 1. Coming!" Duck shrieked.

"Found you, Chicken! Found you, Sheep!" Duck quacked. "I'm the winner!"

"That was quick!" Chicken and Sheep said.

"That's because I'm an expert seeker," Duck said.

But Owl was still sitting in his tree. He had seen all of Duck's peeking!

"Duck!" Owl said. "You are a cheat! I saw you! You were playing hide and peek!"

At first, Duck tried to deny it. But all the animals knew how wise Owl was.

Now Owl, Sheep and Chicken didn't want to play hide and peek with Duck.

So they went back to the farmyard.

Duck was left on her own at the pond.

She splashed around for a while, but it wasn't much fun. She missed Sheep, Chicken and Owl.

I wish I hadn't peeked, she thought.

Duck set off for the farmyard.

"I'm so sorry for peeking!" she said to Sheep, Chicken and Owl.

Then she went back to her pond.

Sheep, Chicken and Owl crept back to the pond. Duck was so happy to see them.

"Happy birthday, Duck," they said. "Would you like to play a birthday game with us?"

"Oh yes," Duck said. "I'll be seeker."

This time, she didn't peek at all!